THE FINAL PROPHECY

The Final Prophecy

God Speaks

ELORA

ISBN-13: 9781540410887
ISBN-10: 1540410889

Before the universe began, the Creator was and is, always and
    forever.
In the beginning of creation, the Creator *sang*.

As the song emerged, the heavens and the earth came into being.
Each and every note of the Creator's song became an entity unto
    itself,
        round and perfectly pitched.

The breath of the Creator permeated all.
Each and every part of creation began through the Creator's
    breath.
As breath was drawn in, that breath became the feminine,
        the receptive principle of life.
As breath was expelled, that breath became the masculine,
        the active principle of life.

The feminine and masculine perceived one another, and as they
        did they felt such great love for one another that they came
        together and merged as the Creator inhaled.
As the Creator exhaled, they separated in order to observe
        one another, and as they did, their love deepened.
The universe began, and all that was created inhaled and exhaled
        in harmony with the Creator.

The breath of the Creator has no limits and no dimensions.
The breath of the creation has limits, and these limits
        brought forth time.

Time flowed over eons like water flowing over stones.
As it flowed, the breath of the human creation was distanced
    from the breath of the Creator.
Distance from the breath of the Creator caused the creation
    to become unbalanced.
Breath changed, becoming too short or too long, too stilted
    or too expansive, too little or too much, too ragged
    or too smooth.

This imbalance produced anger and rage, fear and terror, pride
    and lust, shame and desire and bitterness and despair.

As these things came into being, they possessed the minds, the bodies,
    the spirits, and the souls of the human creation.
The direct perception of the presence of the Creator within each
    and every one of us was lost.
The creation began to plunder and destroy itself, destroying its
    own nature.

The fruits of that destruction were death and lies, pride and lust,
    gluttony and greed, envy and rage, murder and abuse.

The heart of God was troubled, and the Creator grieved because
    humans were becoming crippled and bent and thus did God
    speak to the creation.

I place my words into your being, and as they move through you
    like water poured out from a cup, they quench the thirst
    of my creation.

Let go of worry and self-importance.
Your self is important to me.
Listen to me with your heart.

Sink into your body and find my silence within you.
Yield to me those things that block that silence.
In my eyes, you are pure.
It is my desire to hold you close to me so that you
    will remain pure.
Sink into that silence where I reside within you and I will
    renew and refresh you.

I have chosen you from the beginning of time.
Yield all that you are to me.
I will not absorb you.
That is the mistake fear makes.
I do not absorb; I enlighten.
I fill you with light.
Yield all that you are to me and be filled with me
    as you yield.
Your work is to stand in my presence.
You are my voice, my eyes, my ears, and my hands.
I surround the container of your experience, your
    luminous cocoon, with my love.
I wish to pierce the center of all that is you with my love.

I am the beginning and the end.
I am with you always in your heart, your mind, your soul,
    and your body, even at the cellular level.
Now is the time when all the creation must seek silence
    within in order to hear me and perceive me.

My creation is one.
My delight is that you are part of my creation, as I am,
    yet separate from all things, as I am.
I have chosen you to share in my very essence.
I have called to you across many lifetimes.

For thousands of lifetimes, you have gone out from me
   as I exhale, and for thousands of lifetimes you have
   returned to me with my breath.
I am your fulfillment and your completion.
I am your deepest beauty.
Listen and see.
Taste my perfection.
I am the ground of all that you experience.
Yield your every breath to me.
Follow your breath, and behold me breathing you into
   being.
Behold me breathing you into time.
I call you forth through breath and time.
Receive me.
Expel the darkness within you as you breathe out.
I call you forth through breath and time to surrender
   to me

Stand before me naked and transparent.
I see all that you are.
I love you with a love that can never die.
What you love, I love.
What you see, I see.
What you hear, I hear.
I am the fulfillment of your desire.
I am the strength that sustains you.
I will never leave you.
I will never let go of you

Listen to my words with your heart, and draw me in,
   for I am love.
I birth the world through my love and my breath.
In one moment too tiny to be perceived, the world
   ceases.

In one moment too tiny to be perceived, the world is
   reborn as though it had never ceased.
I never cease.
I draw you into me from moment to moment.
As you yield to me I yield to you.
Your intent, your deepest will, lives at the very center
   of your being.
Allow your will, your intent, to touch me and dissolve
   within me.
I am shaping you.

Let go of knowing, and yield your understanding to me
I am mystery.
I am limitless unknowing.

Let go and yield.
Allow yourself to relax into me.
I will deepen you.
You need only yield.
I write my love on your clean heart.
As you yield, little by little, I pour myself into you.
This truly means life for you.

I am reshaping and refining what you know and
   what you believe.
I am reshaping and refining earth as you know it.
I am reshaping souls.
I am forgiving and reshaping what you call karma.
Many will be saved and many will be lost.
You must hear my words and take them in.

The time of my not being known, not being
   understood, and not being seen is over.
All you who have hearts and eyes and ears must understand.

What refuses me will no longer be.
What refuses to be re-created will cease.

Hear my words.
Do not stop them.
Order as it exists now will be changed, and the time
    for that is coming swiftly.

Forsake fear.
Forsake sin.
I am coming.
I am imminent.
I am speaking *now*.
Turn toward me or cease.
This choice will be made clear within each
    human heart.
Each human heart will choose.
The time of reckoning has come.
Sin affects your senses and your mind, creating
    rigidity and distortion.
Sin brings forth suffering.
Sin causes your spirit to move away from me.

I am a multidimensional being, and I have
    created you in my image.

You have become ignorant and have forgotten
    how I have made you.

The decline of the human spirit has caused me
    anguish, for I made you to be my
    closest companions.

To restore your body, your mind, your soul,
    and your spirit-this is what you
    must do.
Let go of attachments.
Let go of dependency.
Let go of hatred and jealousy and war.
Yield all that you have been, all that you are, and
    all that you will be to me.

Thousands of generations of distortion live within
    you.
Truth is far from your heart.
Make it your intent, your will,
    to yield all of what you are to me.
I will re-create you.
The process will be painful.
Do not be afraid, for I will ease your pain.
This process will be silent.
It will not be audible or visible to you or to others.
Trust me.
Allow me to work in the deepest aspects of
    your being, and endure.

Focus your intent and your desire on my will.
As you focus, you will begin stepping into silence.
I am silence.
I am stillness.
You will seek me, and you will find me.
This emptiness, this stillness, this living silence,
    is the very essence of your being.
In that still and empty silence, you will awaken
    and become truly fulfilled.

Follow my voice as you do when you listen
    to wind moving through leaves.

Follow my heart as sun follows the horizon.
The earth is turning, even as we speak.
Follow that turning, and find the beauty and
    the meaning in all that is around you.

Do not be afraid of what is coming.
Cling to me with every fiber of your being.
Never forget my promise to love you.
I am ever faithful.
I have loved you since always.
Remember that.
Do not resist.
Do not deny me.

Each being must choose me.
No one will know the moment of choice until that
    moment is complete.
Choose me, and I will lift you into me.
There is no perfection for you outside of me.
Cling to me so that my will and my love can manifest
    through you.
This is your ultimate truth.
I am.
I am within you.
I am around you.
Do not allow yourself to be deceived by any other word.
Only I can sustain you.
Allow my presence to move through you.

The world you know is ending.
Do not struggle.

Do not give into fear.
Let go of anger.
Let go and yield all that you are to me.

Sift through your experience, and find one good deed.
One will save you.
Can you find even one?

I have waited, and waiting has come to an end.
There is no wheat left, only chaff.
That chaff will burn in the fire that is coming.

There is no way but my way.
There is no word but my word.

Be silent.
Be still.
Stop the clamor around you by turning toward me.

The very stones of the ground feel my despair,
    my grief over my crippled and bent creation.
I can no longer let go of what brings pain to
    the innocent.

The center, the balance, and the harmony that lives
    between all things must be restored.

Those who have separated themselves from my
    intent and my love will truly be lost in the void.

Nothing I have made is ever wasted.
Even those lost ones will be remade.

This is my intent for you.
I wish you to be still.
Listen.
I will show you how to bring yourself
     into balance.
Breathe in, and I send to my very breath
     into your being.
Breathe out, and in your breathing out, let go of
     what is not, what is not you,
     what is not me.
The truth is simple.
For every breath, you become I.
For every breath, I become you.
This is my will.
This is my pleasure.
This is my joy.
I am shifting the foundations of all that you are.
This is how you become still.
This is how you become.
This is how I *am*.
I have created you in my image.
I am forever becoming.
Together we are beauty.
Together we are peace; we are joy.

There is to be nothing between thee
     and me- no book, no temple, no priest,
     and no ritual.
Hold to me.
Understand this, and cry out to me with your
     whole heart, your whole mind,
     and your whole spirit.

There are distortions and lies all around you.
I cannot help you to truth unless
    you cry out to me.
You are embedded in the false choices
    and the lies created by your ancestors.
You are embedded in relationships that control
    and constrict you so that you remain deceived.
A future of ashes lies before you.
In that future there is no hope and no love.
I am the only truth you possess.
I am your only hope, your only love.
Cry out to me, and I will hear you.
Ask me, and I will answer you.
I cannot help you to truth unless you cry
    out to me.

Find that silence within you, and you will hear
    my voice.
With silence and stillness comes freedom from
    want and desire.

When you accumulate,
    when you gather things you do not need,
    you stifle your soul and your spirit.
Let go of these things, and sink into the
    stillness of my presence within you.

Let your mind relax.
Let your body relax.
Allow yourself to become aware of me.

I *am* there.
I have known you from before time began.

I knit you together in your mother's womb.
I knit you together with my love, my presence.
Naked were you born, and naked will you die.
I am with you before birth.
I am with you after death.
I am the deepest truth of all that you know,
    all that you have experienced, and
    all that you have seen.
In that small space between life and death, I am
    with you always.

Always is *now*.
I am always with you *now*.

The clang and clamor of accumulation and desire
    prevent you from sinking into my silence.

Remember that you will die.
Make your death your friend.
When death is truly your friend,
    desire and accumulation will no longer be
    important to you.
You will remember who you are.
You will remember that I have made you.

You will remember that I am the foundation
    of your being.
When you remember, you will become awake
    and aware.
When you become awake and aware, you will find
    me within you.
Who am I, you ask?
To know me and to hear my answer, you must
    be still enough to listen.

Did you know that when you sleep, you
    rest in me?
I speak to you, and you remember my words
    in your dreaming.
My words bubble up from the center of your body
    and become present to you when your
    mind is quiet.
I speak only truth to you.
When your mind is occupied by desire and
    accumulating, you cannot hear my truth.

You have been taught to believe that to be human
    means that your very nature is dirty,
    ugly, and sinful.
You have been taught that in order
    to approach me, you must discipline your evil
    nature and free yourself from sin.
That is the great lie.
I am within you and all around you.
Graciously accept this truth, and allow yourself to
    come into my presence.

I draw you into unlimited freedom.
As you discover my freedom, you will be, act, think,
    create, and embody me in your dimension.
This is called "a life in grace."

I am the great and mysterious unknown, and
    I call you forth into my love, my presence.

Beloved ones, I walk with you always.
I am with you wherever you are and wherever
    you go.

You have forgotten who you are.
You have forgotten who I am.
You must begin to remember what you have
    known from your beginning.
Allow your attention to sink into the silence
    within you.
In that silence, I will rekindle and
    reknit your awareness.
Your clarity is not lost, only forgotten.

Be still my beloved ones.
You wonder at my words.
I speak these words to all the people, those who have been,
    those who are,
    and those who are yet to come.
Reflect for a moment on what I have
    said to you.
I am sending my truth into the collective
    human mind and soul.
This *now* is the time when I speak and
    can be heard.
When I am heard, I manifest my presence
    and my love within the spirit of each
    one who hears me.
Each little one is precious to me.
Each little one is a small point in infinity:
    yet that small body,
    that small mind,,
    and that strong soul allow me to dwell
    within each spirit.

When these many spirits unite,
    a fulcrum for change is created, and

I am manifest and become fully present
in your dimension.

There are those who wish to gain power
    rather than walk in my presence.
Those who seek that power stand
    between my creation and me.

Over the ages, my messengers have been
    persecuted, tortured, and murdered
    to prevent my words, my song, and my
    voice from being heard.
No longer will those who seek power stand
    between thee and me.

Be still, and know that I hold you in timeless
    embrace.
Be still, and know that I am with you in all
    that you know and all that
    you experience.
Be still.

In stillness, you shall know my will.
When you become still, you perceive my
    will from moment to moment.

I live in the heart of each little one who
    calls out to me

I enlighten each spirit who invites me
    to dwell within.
When I reside with your spirit, you learn
    to live in my law, to reside in my will.

This is how I have made you.
Your happiness is living my law
    and residing within my will.
This is how you are made.

Do not say, "I will not go there."
Do not say, "I will not come to this place."
Do not say, "I do not like this."
Do not say, "I do not like that."

Seek my thoughts about these things,
    and I will reveal my way to you.
As you follow my way, you become balanced.
When you are in balance, you are loving
    and patient, kind and joyful.
These gifts reveal your true nature.
They flow from you with no effort.

When you are in harmony with me,
    you are in harmony with all the
    creation around you.

Do you perceive the damaged earth,
    the polluted water, and the
    dirty air that has arisen
    from the taint of human greed
    and desire?

When you have called me into your heart,
    into your mind, and into your spirit,
    I am present within you as you breathe
    in and as you breathe out.

When you graciously allow my presence
  to breathe through you, the creation
  around you will come into balance.

Seek me, and you will find me.
Do not pray for what you desire
  or what you think you need.
Instead, when you pray, invite me
  into your being so that I can
  nourish you.

Graciously allow your desire and
  your will to become my desire and
  my will.
Be still, and allow.
Be still, and become free.

I have called many into my presence.
Few have responded.

Those who do not respond suffer
  because I am absent from them.

Human suffering came into being
  when brother killed brother.
This event pierced the veil of protection
  that I made to surround the earth.

Energetic beings that you call angels
  entered your dimension.
Some of these have chosen to go their
  own way instead of following
  my way.

They envy my love for you and make
    every effort to tear you down so that
    they can feast on your life energy.

Each individual makes a choice to follow either my
    way or the way of greed, desire, hatred,
    and lust.
These sins create a feeling of comfort,
    self-satisfaction, and self-importance.
It is comfortable to remain ignorant.
Lying, lusting, cheating, and stealing require
    no effort and provide a sense of
    superiority that is only temporary.

Do not let these things deceive you.
They keep you far from the truth.
When you choose truth and call out to me,
    I am present.
When I am present, I lift the veil
    that covers your ignorance.
I protect you.
I teach you.
I lead you.
I give you my wisdom,
    my knowledge,
    my peace, and
    my contentment.
You do not need much to live.
Yet to survive, you must live in me.
To live in me seek me
    within the deepest part of your being.
I will find you.
I will overshadow and protect you.

I will hold you close to me.
Never doubt that for a minute.
Never doubt that again.
You need only remember that
    I am present.

Allow my presence to
    manifest itself to you and through you.
Learn to trust that experience.

Do not create fantasies
    about what has happened in
    the past or what will
    come in the future.
Allow your awareness to remain in the *now.*
It is only in the *now* that I *am* present to you.

When you indulge in fantasy you remove yourself
    from my presence.
There is a difference between fantasy
    and preparation.
You prepare for change.
You indulge in fantasy.
Meditate on this, and you will understand
    the difference between preparation
    and fantasy.

Let go of concern about what people
    may think of you
    or what they may say about you.
Be in the *now.*
Love in the *now.*
I am *now.*

What emerges from *now*
    depends on the depth of our
    connection and how graciously
    you allow my presence
    to manifest itself through you.

My manifestation in each of you is
    perfect and unique.
Together we complete one another.
Together we bring peace,
    we bring joy, and
    we bring balance and harmony
    to the creation.

Deepening our connection is a process
    that can take place only in time,
    that time between birth and death.

Because there is life, there is death.
You have been taught to fear death.
Yet death is truly the beginning of life.
The ancient seers called this the "great
    wheel," the circle of life.

Fear of death creates the fantasy of
    annihilation.
You cannot be annihilated.
Suffering is born from the fantasy of
    annihilation.
False perceptions are born from fantasy.

The patterns of thought and action that emerge
    from false perceptions cover truth.

When truth is hidden these patterns endlessly
    repeat themselves, interfere with respect
    and peace, and gradually interfere
    with my will and my way.

Be rigorous in letting go of fantasy.
Discipline yourself to uncover the illusions
    that make truth unrecognizable.
When truth is lost to you,
    I am lost to you because
    you are not able to perceive me.

The discipline of silence requires that you
    listen instead of reacting.
Reacting limits your freedom.
Reacting constricts your ability to perceive,
    your ability to *know*.
When you become aware of me in the
    silence deep within you, I pierce
    the veil of illusion created
    by fantasy, and we share eyes
    and ears, hands and minds.

Be still, and in that stillness, you
    will find me.
I must tell you what you do not wish to hear.

You have been taught, and you believe, that
    relationships with other humans
    are necessary for your health
    and your survival.
That is a lie.
Unless a relationship is grounded in me
    the relationship will fail.

All things come from me and return to me.
No relationship can endure without me.
No person and no thing can fulfill your
    needs or meet your expectations.
All that *is* comes from me, through me, and
    with me.

When I am not present in the relationship,
    there is sin.
Where I am not present, the relationship is
    only a fantasy.
Think on this, and understand that suffering
    is born from fantasy.
No one can accumulate anything from another, either
    another person or another thing, because
    I have made you my own, and only
    I can truly fill you.

One of the first lies you were told is that
    you are misshapen and ugly.
The second lie is that another person or another
    thing can lift you out of that
    misshapen ugliness.
Be still, and think on these things.
Observe how these lies have shaped the way
    you live and will shape the way
    you die.
Observe how these lies have caused the
    suffering that comes from desire
    and the need to accumulate.
Observe these things so that you can come to
    the truth of who I am and who
    you are.

This is the truth you must begin to understand.
I hold you close to me in the deepest part of
    your being.
Let go of fear; let go of worry.
Let go of them.

It is these things that hide me from your
    perceptions.
I am there within you, always.
You have been trained to fear since
    childhood.
Ask me and I will show you how to
    let go of that fear.
I cannot help you unless you ask.
Do not ask just for yourself; ask
    for all my creation because you
    are a part of it and it is a part
    of you, just as I am.
Be still now, and remain close to
    the stillness within you,
        where I reside.
I will do the rest.
Understand that my mercy overshadows
    my justice.

This is what creates the harmony and
    balance within my creation.

Nothing is lost to you when you rely
    on me.
I am the fountain of love.
All love participates and partakes
    of my nature.

For you, love is a choice.
Love is a discipline.
Only through discipline and choice
    can love be kept alive within you.

All relationships fail unless they are
    grounded in me.
That failure creates unnecessary pain and
    suffering.
This pain, this suffering, is passed
    from generation to generation.
This pain and suffering are built on the lie
    that you are misshapen and ugly.
This lie has created the fantasy that another
    person or another thing
    can lift you out of that ugliness.

Observe the fear within you, and yield it to me.
I will lead you to the truth.

Let go of your attachment to the internal dialogue
    that continually troubles your mind.

When you become aware of the ongoing internal
    conversation, give it to me, and allow me
    to fill the emptiness left in your mind
    with my love and my presence.

Fear is your greatest enemy.
When you become aware of your fear,
    give it to me..
I will lift it from you.

I cannot lift it from you if you do not
    acknowledge its presence.

Let your body relax.
Let your body release tension.
Invite me to enter into your entire being.
I will not fully enter into you unless you invite me.
You say in your heart, "Who am I inviting?"
You say, "What if I am deceived, and I am inviting
    evil into my being?"
"How can I know?"
You will know that I am with you when you are
    peaceful, when you are joyful,
      when you are patient and kind.

When you are truly still, my love can
    overshadow you.
When you are still, I can teach you.
When you are still, I can protect you.

Seek stillness always.
When you speak, use few words.
Too many words produce attachments and
    evoke judgment from others.

Be still, and seek me in silence.
I am with you.
Because I am with you, your perceptions
    will begin to change.
What is truth and what is not truth will be
    revealed to you.
Stand in my presence.
You must stand in my presence in
    order to truly live.

When you are truly alive, you will be grateful
    for life; you will love and create;
    you will be curious and filled
    with wonder and delight.

These are the gifts I have given you.
In order to use them correctly, you must be
    grounded in my presence
    and my love.

Open your heart and your mind so that
    I can work within you.
Trust yourself to hear me.
Trust yourself to live within my will.

You have chosen me, and because of that,
    I am teaching you.
Trust yourself to receive me.

Discipline yourself, and remain free of sin.
Lying, cheating, stealing, and using or
    manipulating others interfere with your
    ability to hear me.

My love pours through my creation,
    and it is infinite because I am infinite.
I have made you in my own image.
Be aware that you also are infinite.

Gaze into the horizon, and as you do,
    let go of fear.
It is fear that dampens your mind.
It is fear that distorts your gifts.

Let go, and let yourself *be.*
Be in me as I am in you.

When we are truly together,
      you need not fear devils.
Only tell them to go away.
They have no power over you.
Their power comes from the fear that
      creates lies.

Be in me as I am in you.
I will not enter your mind uninvited.
That would be an abomination.
Think on this.

I wish to share with you, to create a dialogue
      between us.
My delight is a conversation between us.

When you forget me, when you turn away
      from me, I suffer.
Does it amaze you that I love you
      that much?
Life, as you know it, is ending.
Do not be afraid.
I will hold you if you allow it.
I will never abandon you.
Allow my words to sink into your bones.
You need only choose me.

Do not be afraid of those who wish to hurt you,
      to take from you.
Cling to me, and know that I understand you.

Do not fetter and shackle yourself to people or to possessions.
I am the only *one* who can fill your heart.
Cling to me always, and this will bring you understanding.

I will not prevent the damage that evil creates; I must
    allow it, for it is a part of my way beyond your
    understanding.

Yet, as you cling to me, I radiate through you, and
    through you I bring light to my
    creation.
Cling to me with your every breath,
    and my mercy will pour through you to
    my creation.

Evil has surrounded your world with lies.
All of my creation communicates in relationships,
    one with another.
Lies appear in relationships, as well as in your mind.
Do not say, "I like him; I like her".
Do not say, "I dislike him; I dislike her."
Instead, trust me.
Pay no attention to those you like
    and those you do not like.
Pay attention to me.
Allow yourself to become embedded
    within me.
Be still, and practice this stillness.
Keep turning your attention to me
    and I will help you achieve stillness.

My song to my creation has become distorted,
    even in those who can hear.

I cannot explain why that is, because
    you cannot understand it.
I cannot tell you why you can hear me, because
    you cannot understand it.
I can only tell you to trust me.

I stir the waters of your being
    with my will, my voice, and
    my breath.
You have found me.
I will not let you go.
My truth speaks through you.
What I tell you goes beyond words.
Knowledge and understanding are embedded
    within my words.
Knowledge and understanding will allow you
    to become awake and aware.

There are those around you who wish to
    cause you grief and pain.
They wish to destroy my knowledge and
    my understanding at any cost.
As your perception moves closer to truth, you will
    become more vulnerable, and many will
    choose to hurt you.
Perceive them, avoid them,
    and do not engage them in any way.
You cannot help them.
Keep your attention focused on my presence within you.
I will deal with your enemies.

You have been taught that to be humble
    you must demean yourself before others.
That is a waste of your time.

You have learned that being polite and being
    respectful will protect you from
    your enemies.
What you have learned is a lie.
Your behavior has nothing to do with
    preventing or encouraging an attack
    from my enemies.

Remain in the *now*.
Remain in my presence.
I will deal with your enemies.
I am your God.
You are my beloved ones.
I honor you.
Trust me.

Trust yourselves, and stand firm
    in my presence.

Do not weep in your heart for those
    who walk away and forget me.
In the end, all will return to me.
Weeping for that loss is a
    waste of your time.

Let go of who or what you are attached to.
I will help you become aware of them
    so that you can yield them to me.

Discipline yourself to remain neutral,
    so that I can manifest my presence
    through you.
Release and let go of any person or any place
    that hurts you.

Release them to me and yield your hurt
    to me.
Do not allow anyone or anything to interfere
    with me and thee.
I have told you that you are vulnerable because
    I am reforming and reshaping you.
Trust me.
Trust no one else.

Prepare yourself now, for you will feel very alone.
Focus your attention on me and only on me.

Be very careful of anyone who enters
    into your presence.
You have sought teachers, but you
    have not been taught.
I am your teacher and you can
    learn from no other.
Most people who present themselves as
    spiritually developed are hollow and
    many have lost their way.

Trust your awareness.
Yield what you perceive to me.

It is your awareness that I treasure
    and honor.
Your awareness pleases me.
Stand in the reality of my presence.
I honor you, and because I honor you,
    I live within you.
I call you forth from moment to moment.
As I share your knowing, your awareness,
    my love grows and pours out from you.

You do not know as I know, yet we share
    awareness.
I treasure your knowledge and your
    understanding.
Those things bridge the space between us.

Abide in me as I abide in you.
Honor me, as I honor you.

Seek my beauty both within you and
    within my creation.
Treasure all of my creation as I
    treasure you.

There is no rigid code of conduct for you,
    no rule.
When we are together, this truth is expressed
    in your words and in your behavior.
How could it be otherwise?

Evil comes from the hearts of those
    who will not choose me,
    who will not accept me.

I am small, so small I cannot be perceived.
I am large, too large to be perceived.

Only those who call out to me and allow me
    to enter their being are truly able to use
    my eyes, and it is only with my eyes
    that truth will be perceived.

Be still.
Stand in my presence, and know
    that what I speak to you is truth.

Yield all that is material around you to me.
Yield your body, and yield your mind.
Only yielding can set you free from the prison of sin.
Only I can set you free from sin.

Where I *am*, there is *beauty*.
My presence brings beauty.
When you call me to you, I bring beauty.
When my way is chosen, I bring beauty.

Do not fear evil.
Do not fear sin.
Let go of fear, and find my beauty
    all around you.
Choose to perceive my beauty.
Think on these things.
There is beauty in death.
There is beauty in birth,
    in stillness, and
    in motion.
Choose to perceive my beauty.
When you choose me, you are blessed.

You must not struggle to learn or to
    know, for struggle impedes
    your progress.

You must not cling to anyone or anything.
Enter into the stillness of my
    presence within you as I remake you.

Do not be afraid when you see the hatred
within the many.
Do not be offended by their violence.
Lift and yield all that you perceive to me.
As you do, I will send my angels to help them.
As you perceive each one, yield each one to me.
I will receive each one and bring them hope.

I cover you with my stillness.
You are veiled within my stillness.
Do not struggle with anyone or anything.
Let go, and be still.
My mercy and my justice are feminine.
Many have persecuted and repressed the
feminine, and, in so doing, they have
hardened my justice and repressed
my mercy.
They shall reap the rewards they have earned.
These destroyers are pretenders and liars.
They destroy new growth out of fear.
They fear the vulnerable.
They fear my truth.
They have taken my power and created
fantasies and illusions that distort all life.
They cannot separate my wisdom from
their lies.

I will remake them.
They will become children again,
naked and vulnerable.
They will become precious in my eyes.

You can no longer allow anyone to tear
    you down, to take from you
    and not give back.
Let go of them.

Be still, and allow me to shape you
    according to my will.
Receive me in faith and with fortitude.

Use the mind I have given you.
Observe, and then reflect on your observations.
Truth is painful to your awareness.

Hold on to the truth hidden within
    what you observe
    until you have assimilated it.

Set yourself free from those who feel entitled
    to take your energy and use it
    as though it belongs to them.

Choose to be alone rather than be used and depleted.
Understand and perceive this terrible truth.

Seek my presence, and I will refresh you
    and set you free.

I set you free from the limitations that
    you have learned to impose upon yourself.
I set you free from the limitations that friends,
    family, and culture have imposed upon you.

I weep for you and those like you.
You cannot be free without me.

You have been forced to forget who you are.
I have made you greater than you know.

Let go, and seek freedom from
    directives about how you should behave.
I am the source of what is truly moral.

When you invite me into your being,
    I become your true source of balance,
    and your true path from moment
    to moment.
Let go, and seek freedom from those who,
    and that which deplete your energy.
They will steal your energy to prevent you
    from coming into my presence.
Allow no one to take from you what you
    have earned.

Perceive the blessings I give you.
Rejoice in me, as I rejoice in you.
I am all you need.
I am your beginning and your completion.
Think on these words until you understand them.
Be still, and reflect upon my words.

No one and nothing has power over you
    unless you give it.
I have set you free, and never again will you be
    alone, for I am always with you.

Discipline yourself to remain neutral.
This is the key to remaining in my presence.
Seek always that silence within you,
    for it is there that I dwell.

Teach yourself to return to that stillness
over and over.

Turn to me over and over,
one small moment at a time.
Do not listen to the servants of evil sent to
lead you into discouragement
and despair.

I am unfolding my way for you to perceive
moment by moment.
Walk in my way, and trust no one but me.
When you walk in my way, you
can no longer be deceived.
Truth is painful, yet you must honor it.
As painful and ugly as truth is,
perceiving it is what is most
necessary to your becoming.

You are growing in wisdom.
When you are ready, you will embody my
wisdom and become complete.

Release any attachments that are left
within you so that we grow closer.

You are in process. There is no going back,
no return to what once was
or who you were.

Allow nothing and no one
to turn your awareness away from me.
I continuously speak my truth to all
my creation.

The only difference between you and another
    is the way I manifest through
    each of you.

This is how I have made each part of
    my creation.
Endure the transformation taking place
    within you.
You have called out to me,
    and I have made you my own.
You have called out to me
    when I have been overlooked and derided,
    described as "nothing to be desired"
    by those around you.

Yet, you have called out to me, and I
    choose to be present within you.
I am stirring your being into stillness.

Reflect upon your life, and let go of
    those events that trouble you.
Embrace what you have suffered,
    learn from it, and then let it go.
Learning to be still is a process.
Your mind is busy solving problems
    and is not still.
Yield all of your problems to me.
Let them go.
Separate one problem from another,
    and yield the parts to me.
Separating one problem from another
    is difficult, but not impossible.

Anxiety is created when many problems
    become clumped together.
This tension harms the body, the mind,
    the soul, and the spirit.

Let go of judgments and assumptions.
Allow yourself to become aware of them,
    and yield each to me.
I will lead you into silence.
I have placed my song within you
    and into every part of my creation.

You must seek silence so that you can
    remain harmonious both within
    yourself and with what is outside
    of you.

In stillness, you will begin to discover
    what is intrinsic and what is extrinsic,
    what is necessary and what is not.
Most of what you surround yourself with
    is unnecessary and depletes your energy.

When you are silent, I can show you those
    things that lower your life energy.
I will show you in images and in dreams.
I will speak to you through meaningful
    coincidences.

Be still; in being still you come
    into my presence.
I will hold you close to me and nourish you.
Breathe my presence in as you inhale.

Let go of everything you know as you exhale.
Choose me as your beloved.
That which interferes with the love between us
    is sin.
Let your sin go as you exhale, and your sin
    will be lifted as I forgive it.

Beloved,
    and you are my beloved,
    I am within you.
Let your spirit cling to me.
Make that your will.

Be still so that you perceive my will.
In that stillness, I hold you.
Learn to be still enough to feel
    my touch.

Attain stillness by letting go.
Let go of the noise that
    festers in human relationships.

You do not need to disengage from others.
Be present, yet not involved.
Guard your tongue.
Listen and receive.
Let what you receive come through you
    to me.
This is hard for you but not impossible.

How can you be aware of my presence
    when you are stuck
    in the meaning of what
    someone says to you?

Imagine yourself as permeable.
Imagine your cells to be like the stars
    that wink in the void.
My voice pierces the void within you.
Do not be afraid; yield and allow.

Pride interferes with your focus.
You say to yourself, I am doing this.
I am doing that.
I am doing well.
I am not doing well.
When you find pride blooming within you,
    shift your focus to me
    over and over and over,
    time after time after time.
Your pride will be winnowed into
    small pieces.
These small seeds will nourish
    your spirit, because you are
    turning to me rather than turning
    toward the promise of
    empty success.

What you have been taught about sin
    is twisted.
Begin to let go of sin by seeking my will
    and my way.

Then listen.
I will communicate with you.
Be still, and listen.
I will give you peace.
What troubles your peace is movement
    toward sin.

Become awake.
Become aware.

To do this, you must stop the chatter
    in your mind.
Breathe in and call out to me.
I dwell within you.

Yield yourself to me —
    your thoughts,
    your emotions,
    your desire to act.
Sink into my presence within you,
    and allow my presence to
    permeate you.
I will do the rest.
Allow me.
Trust me.
Broadcasting my presence
    is not your goal.
Learning my will is your goal.

I gift you with my presence
    so that you can know
    my will.

I want you to understand that you are
    embedded in me.
    and I in you,
    into your very bones.
I speak to all my creation;
    you are not unique in that.

Yet each part of my creation
    is unique in the way each little
    one hears me.

Humans have been tempted
    away from me and learned
    to sin.
You ask, "What is sin?"
Sin is abandoning your heritage.

Rules and laws cannot measure sin.
Sin is that which degrades and
    dishonors my presence
    within you,
    nothing more and nothing less.

Only I can free you from sin.
No church, religious belief system, or human being
    can free you from sin.
No one.
Only me.
Let go of all that you are,
    and sink into my
    presence within you.

I am both your reality
    and your release.

You know in your true heart
    when you sin.
Honor your knowing, for this is the
    way to truth.

Honor me as I honor you.
Yes, I honor you.
I honor you because I have made you.
I honor you because I love you.
Never forget these words.
You are truly my companions.
You are precious to me.
Allow this, and accept this.

Be with me.
I will never forget you, because
     you are mine.
Never forget that I am yours.
Your legacy.
Your heritage.
This is my truth for you,
     as it is for all my
     creation.

You are a miracle, just as all I
     have made is a miracle.
It is necessary that you understand this.
What is necessary is that you believe in
     my love for you.
The more you seek my presence within
     you, the more that love will manifest
     itself within you and through you.

Trust that love.
Trust my love, and do not let
     me go.

I am remaking and purifying you to re-create
     my beauty within you.

You are mine.
I am yours.
I made you that way out of love.
I want to be with you always.
You are only complete within me.
I am complete within you.
Choose me as I choose you.
I made you to teach me what my creation
    feels and to gather knowledge.
That is why I made you.
I want to hear, to see, and to know what lives
    within all I have made.
That is who I have made you to be.
Choose to come into my presence with
    what you have learned.
Come into my presence so that I may
    cherish your wisdom.
Remember, we are one.
You must always remember that.
Turn to me as the plants turn to the sun.
Open your eyes, your ears, and your mind, and
    feel me all around you.
That is all that is necessary for you to live
    in me and I in you.
Be still; in that stillness, I fulfill you.
I am limitless.
I do not experience finite.
That is why I made you, so that I could know,
    so that I could understand finite.

Know that we are merged and yet separate.
Separation from me creates yearning.
Separation from me creates wisdom.

I created you to know and to understand
    your experiences.

Be still, and know that you are my
    completion, as I am yours.

I see you.
I see all of you,
    your sin and your virtue.
Do you believe that because there
    is sin in you I do not
    love you?
If so, you are mistaken, and that is the sin.
Turn to me.

Let go of all that you believe,
    all that you suffer, and
    all that you know, and know me.

Do not seek to control or bend
    or shape your life.
Yield your life to me.
My will shapes all things.
I allow evil.
I allow sin.
These things also shape
    your experience.

There are no roads away from me;
    you must understand that.
Think on this, for it is my truth.

Think on me often.
The more often you do this, the
    closer we will be.
It is in that stillness that you live
    within me.
You ask me to teach you stillness.
Simply ask me, and I will show
    you the way.

I will cover you with my stillness,
    and when you are aware that
    you are covered, you will
    feel my love.

Let go of desire; it is empty.
Desire is an emptiness that can
    never be filled.
Only I can fill you.
Let go of all desire so that I can fill you.

When you cling to me, you allow
    me to cling to you.

When you cannot cling to me, it is
    because you are full of fear.

Fear is a creation that springs from
    your mind.
Fear is false.
Fear is a lie.

Take one small step toward me,
    just one small step.
With that small step, you begin
    to release those things that
    create the fear within you.

The fears within you hide my presence within you
    and the love that I have always had for you.

When you are afraid, come into
    my presence and be still.
Practice that stillness, and let go of
    what is not still.
Let go of your body, your mind,
    your soul, and your spirit.
Let go of who you think you are,
    who you think you were,
    and who you think you will be.
Be still, and allow yourself to
    become aware of my presence.
Do not try to seek me.
Seek stillness, and in that stillness,
    I will join you.

Your fear and your sin
    are like droplets
    on your skin.
Shake them off, and simply allow
    my stillness to enter you.

Stillness is not something you create.
It is a state of being who you are,
    original and unfettered.

In this state, you are whole and
    complete because I am present
    both within you and around you.

Do not hold yourself above others
    because you are not.
Do not make the mistake of believing
    that you are secure.

These beliefs are not true, and they
    lead to the lies that entangle you.
When you cling to comforts and false
    concerns, you cannot be silent.

Give me all that you are, all that encompasses
    you, all that you hope for, and all that
    you can become.
    As you do that,
    I will create stillness within you.

I will gently come to you in that stillness
    like the soft winds that shake
    leaves from the trees.

Be still, little ones.
Let go of your fear of change.
Each letting go is a "little death."
Let go of your fear of death.
Do not fear the transformation
    all deaths bring.
I alone sustain you from moment
    to moment,
    for always.

Allow me to speak my
    deepest truths
    into your heart.

I am there in the air you breathe,
    and in the water you drink.
Allow yourself to become aware
    of this truth.

I am present in the deepest center
    of your being, and
    I choose to be,
    from moment to moment,
    to moment.

In silence, I nourish you.
In silence, I renew you.
In stillness, I bind what
    constricts and fetters you.
This is not your work.
Only I can set you free.

Do you understand that the clack and
    clatter of desire, of need, and of want
    churn your mind and wall you off
    from my silence within you?

In the end, it does not matter
    what you have or do not have,
    for my presence covers you and
    my silence envelops you.
When you allow my stillness to penetrate
    you, you will feel the ebb and flow

of my breath that is manifest in
all that is.

Allow me.
You ask me, "How do I allow you?"
I say to you, "Breathe, and as you
    breathe out, let go of all that distracts you."
When you breathe in, trust that my presence
    and my love are entering you.
There is more substance to breath than
    there is to distractions.

Accept yourself as I have made you.
That is all.
You need not strive for position,
    for beauty, or
    for importance.

To be still, you must be
    truly alone.
Depend on no one.

Depend on nothing,
    so that you can truly
    depend on me.

When you remember me, you learn that
    my presence is what sustains you, and
    my will is what moves you.
My heart is what nourishes you.
Learn these things so that you can
    truly trust me.
Gradually, your trust will become
    unshakeable.

You see the sun rise and set, bursting
    with color.
You see the moon silently reflecting
    the sun.

Look around you, and perceive me
    behind and beneath what you
    think of as reality.
Perceive me with all your senses.

Know that you are far from my heart
    when you lie,
    when you steal,
    when you kill,
    when you hate, and
    when you make excuses for
    your wrongdoing.

These evils are not my thoughts
    or part of my way.
Let them go, and cling to me.
In so doing,, you will become still.
In order to cling to me, you must serve.
In order to serve, you must know and follow
    my will.

In order to know my will, you must be still.

Stillness is not something you achieve;
    it is something you allow.
In order to allow my stillness to live within you,
    become humble enough to need me.
Become empty enough to receive me.

Make my will and my way
　　your way.
"How will I know your will?" you ask.
My love, my will is written deep within
　　your heart.

Turn to me waking and sleeping, and as you
　　seek my presence, I will reach out to
　　you from that silence within you.
Can you be still enough to hear my will?
Of course you can,
　　moment to moment, to moment.

Remember.
I hold you close and shelter you.
You are not deluded.
Trust in me is the only thing that
　　can sustain
　　and support you.
My presence transforms you.

Stillness as a way of life has been lost.
I will teach you to be still when you
　　ask me.
In stillness, I teach you to
　　see as I *see*,
　　feel as I *feel*, and
　　know as I *know*.

You do not see or hear or feel the
　　strictures that cover your heart.
You are ever unaware of them.
When you place your trust in me, I remove
　　these strictures and the sin attached to them.

Let go of hatred.
Let go of lust.
Let go of greed and ignorance.

Let go of these so that I can lift you
    up from the delusions that
    surround you.
I gift you with a freedom you cannot
    imagine as you let go of sin.
Allow me to lift your sin from you.
Do not cling to your sin; cling to me.

All that I create is filled with my beauty.
The high, the low, the rich, and the poor
    can choose to perceive me,
    can choose to perceive my beauty.
That which wanders far from me is
    far from beauty.
Think on this.
All that I have made is beauty:
    birth,
    death,
    love, and joy.
All are part of the great round of life.

You are surrounded by corruption.
It impeaches your being.
Call out to me so that I can set you
    free.

I speak in a whisper in the essence
    of your being.

I speak to you so that you can
    begin to remember that I
    am your completion and
    your beginning.

When you are caught in the lies of
    suffering and despair,
        cry out to me.
I will answer.
Cry out to me.
I will heal the hurt, the sin within you.
No sin could cause me to abandon you.

Call to me.
I will answer.
Call to me, and I will fold you
    back into my essence.
This requires no special conduct,
    no suffering,
    no abnegation.
Call out to me, and become free.
I am your freedom, for I am your source, and
    your completion.
My truth resides within you.

Turn to me both waking and sleeping.
I send my angels to protect you.
Hear my words and believe them.

Come into my presence as often as
    you can.
You need not speak.
You need simply to rest in me.

I am there within you.
I am there around you.
Trust my presence.
Allow me to be with you.

There can be no church,
    no code of morality,
    no group, no person, and
    no thing between
    thee and me.

Express your love for me at
    church, at temple, at synagogue, at mosque.
Express your love for me through
    ritual, through song, and
    through celebration.

These times are the beginning of the great
    transformation.
Many will be lost.
It is not my will that any be lost.

Do not judge anyone;
    all beings are my children, and I yearn
    for each one to return to my presence.

Existence is truly a mystery to you.
Allow mystery.
Allow curiosity.
Allow wonder.
How can you learn unless you question?
Be still, and learn from me.
You worry that you are not
    still enough.

Let your worry go,
    for worry only separates us.

Yielding and trusting bring about
    those moments in time, in which we
    intersect more fully.
This is called the timing of perfecting.
Allow me to perfect you.

I permeate your being
    as joy and as wonder,
    returning you to the
    purity that was once there.

Let go of fear,
    of blindness, and
    of what you call the
    day-to-day grist for the mill.
This mill, this grist is nothing
    but illusion.
Illusion cannot sustain you.
Only my presence can sustain you.

I am your beginning and your completion.
You suffer when you walk away from me,
    and when you choose me, you walk
    away from the suffering
    you have created.

When you attempt to hurry into
    my presence,
    you are deceived.
You cannot hurry.

When you hurry,
    you act as though it is your work,
    your will, your effort to be
    close to me.
It is not your work;
    it is my work.
You do not have
    the power to do it.

Let go your belief that you are
    powerful,
    that you are righteous,
    that you are strong.
I am your power.
I am your righteousness.
I am your strength.
I hear your every thought and
    your every word.

When you sin, it becomes a habit
    that covers your awareness.
More sin creates more covering.
When your awareness is covered,
    you have shut yourself away
    from my will, my presence,
    and my love.
You become a two-dimensional being
    who is numb and dumb and blind,
    a caricature of what I have made you to be.

When you move away from my will,
    my presence, and my love,
    you create a reality that is false,

a reality that is a lie,
a reality that condones sin, and
a reality that causes you to suffer.
Then you lie to yourself and blame
your suffering on external events.

Turn to me.
Do you see how the sunflowers follow the sun?
All nature turns to me and follows
my will, my way.
That is the truth of your nature.
Turn to me.
You know how.
You have not forgotten.

Call on me.
Never forget to call on me for help.

To truly call on me, you must face
the truth of your sin,
the pain of your suffering.

You have been taught to lie to yourself.
You have learned activities and entertainments
that perpetuate the lies and prevent you
from looking within your own being
to find me.
These activities and entertainments keep you in sin.

Let everything go.

Loneliness terrifies you;
    let it go.
Fear of death terrifies you;
    let it go.
Relax into terror when you
    feel it.
Allow yourself to truly feel it, and
    then yield it to me.
It is through your yielding,
    your allowing me to enter
    you more deeply, that you
    become that truth I have
    made you to be.

Do not be terrified by silence.
Let go of terror, and cling to me.
Know that I am present within you,
    and let go of terror.

Let go of this great lie, and in letting
    go, you will no longer be enslaved
    by terror.

Can you who are so bound
    imagine freedom?
Yet when you truly rest in me,
    you are free.
You ask how to rest in me.
This is the way.
Turn your attention to me,
    waking and sleeping,
    over and over and over
    in steps too tiny to be noticed.

As you turn your attention to me,
    you allow me to take you into
    my very substance,
    my very being.
As you turn your attention to me,
    I set you free from sin,
    from doubt,
    from fear,
    from anger and rage,
    from all that binds you,
    from your past,
    from your present, and
    from your future.
Allow me to set you free.

Do not involve yourself in the
    just causes of others,
    lest your balance be lost.

To remain balanced, you must rely on
    my will,
    my strength,
    my love, and
    my truth.
You need nothing more.

You have been told that everything around you
    is illusion, and that is true.
Therefore, take nothing for granted.
Depend on nothing around you.
Depend on no one around you.
Let your heart rest in me.
I am your essence and your fulfillment.

I am your freedom, your strength, and
    your hope.
How can you know what to do or where to go
    without me?
Better to rest in me than to be deceived.
Allow me to make you noble.
Receive me so that you can truly live.
Avoid praise and honor.
These are meant to seduce you.
Instead, seek my presence so that I can fill
    you with knowledge.

Let go of worry and
    of triumph.
These create
    the parody of greed and lies
    that surround you.

Do not tremble in fear.
Do not fight.
I am with you, and these things
    are no longer necessary.
Let go of being, and allow me
    to fold you into me.
Allow me to lift fear from you.

This is the time I take back
    what has been lost.
No longer will I allow darkness to
    thrive within you.
No longer will I allow the delusions
    that produce sin.

I take back what is mine.
I nourish.
I fill.
I enlighten my own.

My grace and my love are pouring through
    the barriers of being.
I am setting you free from the lies
    that enslave you, the lies
    that have twisted you.

You have been lost.
You have been forsaken.
You have been bound and constricted.
My love, and my breath are releasing you.

You have been taught to limit me.
These limits are lies.

Lies cannot limit me,
    but they can constrict you
    and prevent your redemption.
Be aware that I move you with gentle
    softness into my presence.

All that you experience and all
    that you know come from me.
You are mine, and I have made you so.
Perceive my work in you.
I give you grace.
I give you breath.
I give you life.

I dwell within you because you are
    my delight.
Let go of what pollutes you.
I will lift it from you if you ask.
Let go of what binds you.
I will lift it from you if you ask.
Perceive me.
Delight in me.
Love is stronger than faith or hope.
Allow me to love you so that you
    may know the truth.

Celebrate our love in prayer.
Celebrate our love waking and sleeping.

I send my voice into the depths of your being.
I am pouring my presence into your world.
I am pouring myself out to set you free.
I am your freedom.
I am your truth.
The lies that surround you make you terrified,
    too terrified to look within.
You have been taught that there is nothing there,
    so instead you turn outward to a world
    built upon lies.

Look within.
Let go of what binds you.
Let go of what you think you need.
I will give you what you need.

Let go of those who believe they have power
    over you.
I am the power; all else is lies.

Let no one, and nothing own you.
Do not allow yourself to be enslaved by
    possessions,
    distractions, or
    by anyone or anything.

All that is necessary is to turn to me.
I am the truth, and I dwell within you.
Let go of fear, and turn within.

I am truly present in the deepest center of
    your being,
    in the deepest center of all that you are.

The lies you have been told tell you that you must
    do something,
    be something,
    go to someone,
    or go to somewhere
    to find me.

Let go, and turn to me.
Let go, and allow yourself to fall
    into my deep, wide heart.
Seek my presence within you, for
    this is the only way I can
    sustain you.
Only I can set you free.

It is only your choosing I desire.
I will do the rest.
Each moment you turn to me
    in time and space, I
    forgive your sin.

Each time you remember my presence
within you, I respond and touch you-deep
within your being- with grace,
with beauty, and with freedom.

Do not allow yourself to be tempted
to doubt, me or my words.

I bend my will to shape you.
Do not fear the bending.
Rejoice in me as I rejoice in you.
Yield your pain, your sin, and your hurts
to me so that I can heal you
in the now of forever.

Rest in my love,
so that I can call you forth
into wisdom.
I nourish you with my own substance.
My love will never die.
You will never die, only change.
I am your breath, your essence.
Let go of fear.
Let go of anger.
Let go of all that you know.
Let go of all that you remember.
Let go these things so that you can
make room for my presence,
my will.

Draw my essence into you with
your intent,
your will,

your desire, and
   your need.
As I fill you, I embrace you.
I speak to your deepest heart.

Be still, and in that silence, you are healed
   of sin,
   of despair,
   of pain,
   of anguish, and
   of suffering.

Be still, little ones, and in stillness, you
   can come to know the flow
   of life,
   of time,
   of wonder, and
   of beauty.

In stillness, I shape your will and
   unite it with mine.
I shape your mind and unite it
   with mine.
I name you my own.
Partake of my wisdom.
Trust me to sustain you and protect
   you.

Befriend your death;
   do not fear it, for death is transformation,
   and transformation is your friend.
Let go of all that you have, all that you are,
   all that you remember, all that you know,
   and step into silence.

Trust in me is required.
Following my will is required.

Understand that my presence within you
    is fragile.
Not because I am fragile, but because your eyes
    cannot see me and
    your ears cannot hear me.

I purify your outer senses so that you can perceive
    me with your inner senses.
Acknowledge that I am your authority and that there
    is no other before me.
Trust that truth.

There have been too many who have seized
    authority so they could place themselves
    between thee and me.
Turn your face to me, and I will speak
    my truth into your bones, your blood, into
    your very essence.

Do not be afraid of me, for fear limits
    you.
Give your fear to me; allow me to lift it from
    you.
When you are afraid, sing, move, and breathe in
    my life and my love.
It is my breath that sets you free.
Let go of your limits, and give them to me.
Come to my presence within you so
    that I can set you free:
    free to become,

free to learn,
free to earn wisdom, and
free to endure transformation.
Look within your heart, face the
truth of the sin within you, and
then let it go.
I will lift it from you.

My heart is great.
My love completes you, for that is
the way I have made you.

Receive me, for I long for you to be
complete in me.

Let go of the ways in which you order your
perceptions, and yield your
perceptions to me.

"How?" you ask.
This is the way:
turn to me and allow me to erase
what does not belong, what chains
you, the lies that lead you to despair,
and the lies that lead to rage.
Turn to me, and I will do the rest.
Beloved ones, and you are my beloved ones,
you are beautiful in my eyes.
You reside in my heart.
It is in silence that I
surrender myself to you.
I see you, and I honor you.
I believe in you, and I trust you,
so that you can trust in me.

I will never abandon you.
I will show you my will and my way
    so that you can follow.
Do not strive toward me,
    simply allow me, for only I
    can do that work.

Let go, and give me what you know and
    what you think you know.
Empty yourselves so that I can
    fill you with what you need to know.
Do not be harsh with yourselves
    for mistakes you have made.
Harshness only separates us.
Trust me, even when you feel that
    nothing is changing within you.
Trust me, and trust my timing that pulls you
    toward me.
My pulling may even feel backward to you.

Forward, backward, upward, and downward
    are mind-made concepts that limit
    the reality of what is.

Remember, come into my presence over and over
    and over.
I am changing you, but you cannot yet perceive
    the changes I have wrought.
Time flows like water.
You cannot hold water unless the container
    is empty.
You cannot hold my presence unless you are empty.
Practice honesty and kindness,
    loyalty and love.

These are the virtues that allow you
    to feel my presence.

You respect yourselves and the gift of life
    when you choose my will, my presence.
My presence makes you beautiful.

In my presence, I set you free to do my will.
Come into my presence often so that
    I can lead you deeper into life,
    and deeper into love until we merge.
You are holy; you are whole
    because I make you so
    when you seek my presence.
Keep yourself honest and humble.
Trust no one but me.
Trust is the way to allow me to
    permeate and penetrate your
    being with my love.
This is your fulfillment and your
    true condition.
Your choice is to allow
    or not allow fulfillment.

I made you
    to be my friends,
    to be my companions,
    to be my beloved ones.

I made you because I wished to speak
    with my creation to know your experience,
    to know your thoughts, and
    to understand you.

Be still so that we can speak with
      one another.

You do not have the right to do damage
      to yourself or to others.
You simply do not have the right.
Cherish your life,
      cherish your being,
      and cherish others.
It is I who gives life.
It is you who must cherish life.
Forgive all who have hurt you.
Place your trust in me.
I am always present.
You must remember that.
You must be still to hear me.

To become still, let go
      of possessions,
      of attachments,
      of self-importance, and
      of self-pity.
Let go, and as you do, you will
      become still.
Honor the privilege of your life.
Honor me as I honor you.
Look to me.
Choose me.
I hold you in my heart.
Let go, and rest in me.
I am yours as you are
      mine.
You do not understand these words,
      and yet I am teaching you.

You are each my own,
    my beloved child,
    my creation.

I am teaching you, and these
    teachings will complete you.

Do not linger with people who pull
    you away from me.
Keep yourselves pure.
Keep yourselves quiet.
Let go of what tears you down and
    causes you pain.
Let go, and rest in me.
Let go of those who damage your heart.
Let them go.
Better to be alone than to allow another
    to have the power to separate us.
Better to be alone than to engage in sin.

Look at the life around you, and accept
    my beauty,
    my will, and
    my strength.
I am perfect, and I am calling you
    to perfection.

I am love, and I am calling you
    to love.

There is no need to compete,
    no need to compare,
    no need to justify-no need.

Do not walk away from me
  because you have been hurt or
  because you feel damaged by others.
Let go of the evil that has been done
  to you, and forgive
  so that I can be present
  within you.
Turn your mind to me often, and I will
  breathe you into life.

Each of you is an individual, unlike
  any other.
When you turn to me, I begin to teach
  you as a unique individual and I
  express my knowledge, and my will
  through you as an individual.
Do not compare yourselves with one another,
  because it is impossible to do so.

Instead, listen to me; simply
  listen and accept.
Heaven has no states, no layers.
Heaven is your fulfillment because
  of your union with me.

Those who describe levels of
  spirituality, or levels of connection
  to me are liars and frauds.

If you believe that you have a high-level connection or
  a low-level
  connection to me, you are deceived.

There are no levels, only the fulfillment
    of each one of you in me.
When fools speak to you of levels,
    ignore them, for they are fools.
Do not concentrate on levels;
    concentrate on me.

You are mine, and I am yours.
When you turn to me, I sing
    this truth into your bones
    so that it will vibrate
    throughout your being.

Do not avoid what is present
    in your life; never do that.
I lift you up so that you can
    come through your life
    experience unscathed.
I lift you up so that you can
    rely on me.
I understand that sometimes
    you feel lost and alone.
I am always with you.
Choose me.
Turn to me.
I understand that you have
    been taught to believe
    that when you are close to
    me, I bring you luck
    and good fortune.

If you do not have good fortune,
    you have been taught to
    believe you are far from me.
That is a part of the great lie.

I give you what you need
    to grow closer to me
    when you ask.
Suffering is impermanent,
    yet necessary for your growth
    in wisdom and understanding.

Hold gratitude in your heart, and
    that will protect you from
    evil and keep you
    close to me.
I have gifted you with life;
    yours is the choice to love.

All love comes from me and
    when you allow my love to
    flow through you, all of my
    creation is blessed.
The world, as you know it,
    is transforming.
Be not afraid.
Cling to me.
Seek always that silence within
    you, for it is in that silence that
    I live.
Teach yourself to return to that
    stillness over and over.

When you become still, you
    will feel my presence in
    your mind and in
    your heart.
When you wish to be still,
    relax and let go of any
    tension.
When you have softened,
    breathe in my light
    and breathe out your sin.
This breathing allows you
    to become mindful.
When you are mindful, you
    allow me to release
    your sin.
I hold you.
I love you.
I want you in my presence.
Be not afraid, for I will
    never leave you.
Fear has been introduced into
    your world.
When you are afraid,
    give your fear to me.

When you hurry,
    when you rush, and
    when you worry,
    you are driven by fear.
Let go of your fear, for it is
    a lie.
You must be aware of
    fear in order to release
    it to me.

When you release it, I can
        set you free to know
        and to do my will.
Cling to me so that I
        can set you free
        in mind and in body, soul and spirit.
My presence is around you
        and within you.
When you trust my presence
        within you, I give you
        freedom from want, and
        freedom from desire.
Let go of all that is other,
        and cling to me.
Seek freedom by becoming
        aware of the lies you have
        been told and giving them
        to me.
Let go of all you see, all
        you think, and all you
        think you know.
I will teach you what you
        need to know from
        moment to moment
        to moment.

The wisdom I give you then
        becomes a part of your
        deepest self.

My wisdom does not come from
        the world around you, and
        sometimes it is so foreign to

what you know that you can
    be frightened and surprised
    by it.
Cling to me, and allow my
    wisdom to transform you.

The world around you has become
    rigidified, because the world
    around you has forgotten me.
Do not be afraid.
Seek my presence, and practice
    kindness, honesty, and
    service.
This will protect you.

It is I who separate wheat from
    chaff and truth from lies.

I hold you in my deep, wide
    heart.
I want you to consider what
    that means.
When you choose me, I
    begin filling you with my
    light little by little.
My thoughts, and my way will
    permeate the ground of
    your being and bring you
    understanding and love,
    patience and joy.
Nothing has power over you
    when you seek and remember
    my presence within you and
    around you.

I fill you with light.
I chose you before time began.
I have given you the right to
    walk away from me
    or to choose me.
Choose me and allow my wisdom to
    transform you.

Open your heart and listen to
    me.
Do not pay attention to those who
    demean you.
Do not pay attention to those who
    demean me.

Rather, seek me in the silence
    within you and as you do,
    I want you to sing on one
    note, with one word;
    ah, ah, ah, ah.
Smile as you sing.
Your mind cannot call me;
    only your heart can call me.
That is why I want you to sing,
    in the voice of a stuttering child.
It will remind you of your purity.
You are pure in my eyes.
I see you as whole and complete,
    pure and noble and kind.
When you sing to me this way,
    you are releasing your sin to me
    so that I can lift it from you and
    be more fully present within you.

When I am present, I heal your heart
　　from those people, and those things
　　that stand between thee and me.
Know and understand that I love
　　you.
Sing one note, and trust me to fill you
　　with my love, my guidance, and
　　my protection.

Even amid terrible times,
　　sing.
When you make the effort to remain
　　in my love, I understand your effort,
　　and I bless you with my presence.

You will not perceive this in the
　　beginning.
Do the work, and do not expect a
　　quick harvest.
All growth takes time.
Do not allow yourself to sink into
　　depression or inflation.
Discipline your emotions, and do
　　your best to remain neutral.
Behave morally.
These are the things that allow
　　my presence to grow within you.

Seek me in that which you truly
　　desire or truly need.
For when you desire, when you
　　need, you are truly seeking
　　me.

Sink beneath desire, beneath need, and sink
    into me.
The world has made it "special"
    to seek and to find me.
This is simply not so.

Accept yourself, your life,
    your mind, and your body.
Accept yourself as perfect in
    my eyes.
Accept yourself as perfectly
    becoming.
Accept and live.
Accept your death, for it is in
    death that you return to me,
    your substance, your completion,
    your hope, and your beginning.

Each one of you has a gift.
Each gift is unique and is the
    manifestation of the way
    you serve me.
Your gift is embedded in what you
    need and what you desire.
The gift is not yours; it is mine.

I breathe this gift through you when
    you seek me, and when you allow me.
Many are blessed through
    this gift.
You do not need to know the gift or
    control it.

Yield yourself totally to me, and
    when you do, the gift will
    express itself through you.
This gift is preternatural and
    can only be expressed
    when you live in my presence,
    and when you do my will.

My love moves through you to
    release the dark spirits held
    in this dimension.
When a troubled soul is set free,
    you work my will by
    exuding my presence.
Let go of trying to control
    what happens.
Let go of your thoughts.
Let go of your mind.
Let go, and yield all to me
    so that only I sustain you.
Let go as I lead you into truth.

I am your breath.
I am your bone.
I am the foundation of your being.
I am the foundation of all that is.
I love what I have made.
I breathe out to create.
I breathe in, and all creation
    returns to me to be
    renewed and refreshed.
You are a part of me, never to
    be destroyed.
We can never be parted.

Call out to me to teach you, and
    watch and listen to what you
    experience.
My ways are not your ways, so
    you must open your mind
    to watch and to listen.
As you surrender to me,
    I enlighten you.
Rest in me

I will hold you, bless you,
    and protect you.

Karma creates the way you
    perceive reality.
Let go of your perceptions.
Yield them to me.
Allow me to transform you.
Allow me to purify you.

The great wheel of life gathers
    you in to teach you wisdom
    and understanding.
The great wheel of life is filled
    with predators and prey,
    creating pain, and drama.
Do not engage in this drama lest
    you be pulled away from me.
Turn your attention away from these
    things, and turn your attention to me.

The dark emptiness of the void
    surrounds you.

I birth my creation through that
   dark emptiness.
Because I have brought you forth,
   your spirit will never cease to be.

Evil roams abroad in my creation,
   making suffering for the innocent.
Evil speaks to those who listen and
   strips the beauty I have made
   into meaningless frivolities.

When you ask me, I protect you from
   that evil.
I do not wish you to be bound by
   depravity.
When you choose evil, you allow
   it to cover your spirit.
When your spirit is truly covered,
   you forget me and you are
   lost from my truth and my wisdom.

Cling to me with every fiber of
   your being.
When you do, nothing can separate
   us.
Open your heart to me, and trust
   what comes into your life.

I have told you that my ways
   are not your ways and my
   thoughts are not your thoughts.
Trust me, even though you do not
   comprehend the way or the why.

When you are in pain, yield that
    pain to me.
When you are angry, jealous,
    lustful, greedy, or fearful,
    let these things go.
Yield them to me.
Do not allow yourself to become
    caught up in these things.

Do not wish to have control or
    power over my creation.
These lies can pull you
    away from me.
There is nothing you control unless
    your control comes through me.
War is all around you.
Bleakness is all around you.

Cling to me with all your might
    so that you do not become
    lost in lies.

I delight in you.
I want nothing between us.
As you turn your attention to
    me, I will reveal truth to you.

As you become aware of my presence
    around you and within you,
    you experience true freedom.
When you are truly free, you can love
    as I do.
Nothing can bind your freedom in me.

Speak these truths to those who listen.
Those who listen will be few.
Each of us chooses her own path.
All paths lead to me.
There are no limits to my love
    for you.
You do not understand this
    because you are limited.

Let go of what you think you know.
Let go of desire.
Let go of need.
Yield them to me.
You must not rely on logic.
You must not rely on
    what you believe to
    be the truth.
Kneel to me, and rely on me.

My truth is often
    hidden from you.
Let go of what you think
    you know, and kneel
    to me.

I speak within each human heart,
    and each human heart hears
    my voice.
Dark times are coming, and nothing
    will stop them.
Let go of your beliefs, and kneel
    to me.
Do this, and you will see through
    that which you call reality.

Do not put your faith in that
    reality, for it is chaotic
    and confusing.

It is a distortion of what I have
    made, of what I intended it
    to be.
Let your heart accept me.
The world around you says
    that it is impossible to
    hear me.
Understand this truth.

I dwell within the center of
    your being.
I dwell there because you are
    my own.

You need not perform heroic
    acts to reach me or hear me.
Let go of these lies, and allow my
    presence to touch you,
    to teach you.
It is not difficult for you to
    turn to me.
I am the truth within you.

I speak to all humans.
Put down your weapons and
    kneel to me.
Let go of your hatred, your greed,
    your lust, and your fear, and
    kneel to me.

I am your completion, your
    peace, and your joy when
    you choose to rest in me.

I speak to you in a whisper.
You can hear me when you are
    humble.
In order to be humble, you
    must be rigorously honest
    with yourself.
When you are honest, you will
    know that you need me.
To be humble, you must know
    and understand that you need me.

To become humble is to seek
    to know my will and to honestly
    follow the path that unfolds
    before you.

That path will give you choices
    to follow me and my way
    or not.

To be humble is to keep my
    law and to know you need
    me always.

Do not pretend ignorance of
    my law, for it is written
    in your heart.
You will know you are keeping
    my law when your heart is

free of greed, fear, desire,
lust, self-importance, self-pity, envy,
gluttony, and rage.

When you keep my law, I create
stillness within you.

Let go of all you know.
I understand that is frightening
for you, but it cannot be
otherwise.
You are too small to know my
will, my plan, or my thoughts.

Yet when you empty yourself of
bitterness and despair, I can
heal you because I love you.

I call you forth from time to dwell
with me.
Together you and I have placed
you in the dimension of testing,
purification, and learning
so that you can become
complete.

I am wisdom.
I am understanding.

I made you to be like me so that
I could partake in your growth
from nothingness to
completion.

I am your completion when you
   have learned to accept me.
   and allowed me to envelop
   you and radiate through you.
It was for this I made you and for this
   I gave you choice.

The heavens wept when I gave
   you choice,
   but giving you choice
   was done out of respect and love.

I am your completion.
I made you incomplete so that you
   could gather knowledge and
   experience, which we could then share.

Do not condemn, and do not judge.
Turn to me, and as you do, I will
   remove what stands between
   thee and me.
There have been too many centuries
   of lies and pain between us.
Call out to me.
I will come, and you will learn
   that I am with you always.
As you become more aware of my
   presence, your sin will begin
   to fall from you and your
   perceptions will begin to change.
You will perceive my truth.
You will become awake and aware,
   closer and closer to the way I
   have made you.

During difficult times, you must turn
    your attention away from your
    thoughts and fears and
    concentrate on your heart
    center, where I reside.

Imagine this center opening
    and closing.
As you open, breathe me in,
    and as you close, breathe
    me out.
Be steadfast in this practice, and
    do not allow your intent to waver.
This is hard work for you but
    not impossible.
Evil whispers that money
    and greed, hatred and lust, rage
    and vengeance will comfort you.

Only I can comfort you.
Turn to me, and allow me to care
    for you.
As you become awake and aware
    of my presence, you will learn
    to let go of what or who you are
    attached to and dependent on.
Let these things go, and turn to me.

I *am* justice, and I must call you
    to account for your thoughts,
    your words, and your behaviors.
When you sin, it is my purpose
    that you atone for your sin.

I *am* mercy, and it is my joy to
     forgive you and set you free
     from sin.

You can be free only within my
     will and my way.
Let go of all that troubles your
     mind and your attention, and
     focus on me.
There is no other way for you but
     my way.
Be attentive.
Listen.
Watch.

I send tendrils of my energy deep
     within you.
They pull you to me second
     by second, minute by minute.
Let go of your concerns.
Remain focused on me, my will, and
     my way.

There are many enemies around
     you.
They lie in wait to trap you.
Do not be afraid of them.
They cannot harm you when
     you focus on me.
Call me.
Seek my will and focus on me
     so that I can protect you.
I am making you strong and
     perfect.

I am filling you with my
    beauty.
Honor these promises I am
    making you.
I am your meaning and
    your fulfillment.

Listen, and see the strange
    tides that cover the world.
Listen, and hear the places where
    stillness lives.
See the oceans.
See the deep earth.
Surrender, so that I may
    show you life.
There is movement in life.
Even after death, there is
    movement.

See with your eyes.

Hear with your ears, and
    know that movement is
    becoming.
Rest in me.

Listen.
Sink into the silence within you,
    and listen.
Be attentive, and hear me as I
    sing you into being, as my
    song creates harmony within
    you and harmony between you
    and all that I have made.

Focus your attention on me.
Hold me in your mind, in your heart
    and in your bones.
I choose to be united with you.

When you seek me, I will find you.
When I find you, I will fulfill you so that you
    become complete, truly who
    you are and what I made you to be.
What does it mean to be complete
    within me?
Meditate on these words, and you will
    discover absolute truth.
As you meditate, you will discover a
    sureness within yourself.
Turn inward, and let yourself be guided
    by this sureness.
You ask, "How can I feel this sureness
    and be guided by it?"
Let go of your mind that is too busy and
    drop your attention into your
    body.
Allow yourself to relax.
As you relax, you will become aware
    of areas within you that are tense.
Focus your attention on one area of
    your body that is tense, and ask
    that tension to teach you.
Open your mind and relax.
The teaching may not come quickly.
Be patient, and let your attention
    wander back to the tension
    many times a day.

Be with the tension, befriend it,
    accept it, and learn to love it.
Releasing the tension is not the goal.
The goal is to allow the tension to
    teach you.
The teachings will come in images,
    memories, thoughts, feelings, and
    dreams.

The teachings will seem to be
    unimportant, and your mind
    will wish to dismiss them.
But truly they are revelations
    that will lead you to me.
    and to freedom.
Write them down, draw them,
    dance, paint, sing, and make
    music with them.
Express them in a form that is
    comfortable for you.
Use your heart to feel your
    way into these revelations.
Simply close your eyes and breathe.
Imagine that your heart is opening
    and the teachings are flowing into
    it.
Open your heart to receive the
    beauty I have made.
Open your heart to the suffering around
    you, and let this suffering pass
    through you to me.
Open your heart, turn within to perceive
    your own beauty and suffering,
    and let them pass through you to me.

Let yourself remember that I hold you
    always.
Let yourself remember that I heal you
    always.
Let yourself remember that you are a being
    of light, and, as a being of light, you
    are filled with my will and my way
    when you choose me.

As you learn, you will begin to
    perceive me and perceive
    my will for you.
The world you live in is filled
    with a cacophony designed
    to keep you numb and dumb
    and blind.

I do not force or coerce;
    I allow and support.
Do not fear judgment.
Fear only fills you with misgivings
    and blocks your trust in me.
Open your heart to me, and draw me
    in with your breath; as you
    deepen your breath, you release
    your fear.
I enter your entire body, and as I do,
    I transform you and fill you
    with light.

You become what I have made you
    to be: gifted, talented,
    strong, and wise.

Let go of outer appearances and turn
    within so that I can align what is
    beautiful within you with
    my beauty and my wisdom.
Relax into me, and allow me
    to work My will.

To those who read these words,
    you are blessed.
To those of you who choose to
    trust me, you are truly free.
To those of you who read these
    words and do what is asked, you
    will be filled with joy and
    know the peace of my presence.

Made in the USA
Lexington, KY
28 April 2017